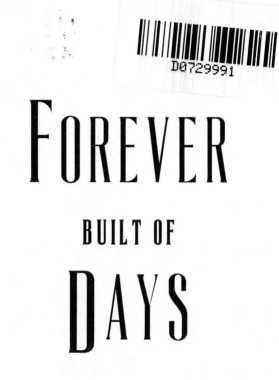

FOREVER

BUILT OF

DAYS

Jessie Witt Pannell

PAGE AND PEN PUBLISHING
MEDFORD, OREGON

PAGE AND PEN PUBLISHING, LLC
PO Box 1911
Jacksonville, OR 97530

Forever Built of Days

ISBN: 978-0-9976916-1-0
Library of Congress Control Number: 2016909363

Interior fonts Cambria and Kingthings Trypewriter

Cover design, art and photography and interior art
© R.C. Davidson 2016
rcdavidsondesign.com

Being with you and not being
with you is the only way I have
to measure time.

Jorge Luis Borges

To Frances Witt: My respect and appreciation travels back in time to the woman I never met, whose brave and tenacious faith birthed my own.

To Rose: Thank you for building a lovely nest from which I could fly.

To Pannell: Whenever you've needed someone to sucker punch you in the face, I have always been there for you. And whenever I've needed someone to hug me, you have always been there for me. I'm so glad I said, "I love you," first!

To Jude, Merrick and Hadassah:
Dear Creatures,
My forever love to nurture you.
My laughter to push you on.
My tears to dry your own.
You are every kind of wonderful.

To Amy, Dallas, Ebeth, Marion, and Ryan:
I can only pay my debts to you with the humble coin of gratitude and affection for your encouragement, advice and support. You have been mirrors to me, reflecting light into dark places.

Let
this be
written for a
future generation,
that a people not yet
created may praise
the LORD. Psalm
102:18
NIV

FOREVER

BUILT OF

DAYS

Table of Contents

one o'clock

A Time to Be Born

Porch Sabbath

The Sabbath of this porch
stands as a gateway
to all I hold dear in the house.
This rocking chair is the sentinel
to greet incoming loved ones.
Alone, I hear their laughter from a distance.
With company, I share in the laughter
and offer my own superior humor.
One day this porch will keep
its Sabbath vigil without me.
Would I keep a Sabbath
without the porch on my own?

Here comes the fall.
My porch begs for attention,
but I must get my sweater.
Alone with my thoughts,
the rocking chair creeks out
the cadence of the years.
It holds my secrets
of whether I laughed enough.
Was I kind?

The winter tries to annoy the porch,
but the porch pays no nevermind.
The chair is more resentful of the cold
because it misses the warmth my backside.
Poor chair.

The spring creeps
its dewy tendrils
onto the porch.
It begs the chair to come play,
rock like the good old days.
The chair does as it is bid
and scoots closer to the edge of the porch
to watch a fern frond unfurl.
Luckily, I'm in the best seat
to watch this display.

And now we welcome another summer.
Here come the children again,
only less child-like.
I hide my mint julep.
Mint juleps go with porches
and sun sacred days
but not with children.
I don't want to share.

Another breeze,
another kiss before the door,
another trip on the stairs,
another scraped knee on the sidewalk.

I rock. I breathe.
Time catches on my sleeve and then races past.
I am limited in so many ways
yet holding onto the mighty purpose of Sabbath.

Ways to Get Naked

Walk Naked
We took a walk and shared the same sky.
Sunlight reflected off your face into my eye,
and I
couldn't dislodge it.

Work Naked
Side by side,
fingers raw,
the fabric of our lives
held together
by our stich in time.

Word Naked
I wrote you a letter.
The paper seized the words that
seeped from my heart,
from me to you.

Art Naked
We listened
to a song we both needed.
It orchestrated a universe where
music ruled the day.
You joined me,
and we let the chorus strip us down.

Eye Naked

The eyes are all nudity, betrayers of burka.
Unshaded, they open your unknown:
violet-gray, unfathomable, unflinching,
trust afforded by an unsecreted innocence.

Cry Naked

I wept enough tears to drown.
The last one came crashing down,
plunging, purged from my conscience.
You caught it.
You held it,
and dried it in the palm of your hand.

Laugh Naked

Laughter, open table around a shared meal,
with a little bottle of wine to sweeten the deal.
Conversation, agree or disagree,
either way you're seeing the real me.
Nodding of heads, rolling of eyes,
listening to stories in their fifteenth reprise.
We laugh again, and I catch your wink,
alone together in the way that we think.

Forgive Naked

A sheer way to undress is to confess a fault.
A sure way to disrobe is to forgive.

Attempt Naked

Show what you are capable of
without embarrassment,
with or without achieving
a hope, a want, a wish, a need,
opened up and laid bare
all because you coerced your will to dare.

Fall Out of Your Fig Leaves

I'm not cowering
behind my hesitations,
nor covering
my heart, mind and soul anymore.
I have lost my virginal dignity,
but I have found a reason to bloom:

I want to be with you.

When Ida was growing up
on the stark homestead,
joy was elusive.
Life was teetering and thin.
The joy was there,
but no one was at leisure
to take hold of it.

She found a man to lie with
after being declared his wife.
She was fifteen
and of acceptable breeding age
when she met Jim at the big dance
at the new Fisher place.

He was hunched and fading
already at thirty
with not much to offer her
but hard work,
a kindly whistled tune,
and hot bread if she would
grind it, knead it, bake it.

She left the soddy,
bare and desolate,
neat and dingy,
with a face straight ahead,
chin held high,
on the back of her favorite horse.

Ginger had always been equal
to carry her on all her adventures,
but Ida didn't know if she could carry her
heavy heart away from her childhood home.

They'd been together once
on their wedding night.
She didn't know what to call it
because an unspoken topic
needed no vocabulary.
It was expected to produce children.
Pride and independence and no self-regard
did not help with this new expectation.

Ginger and Ida arrived at their sudden home.
Jim stepped out to greet them.
She noticed he'd taken pains
to sweep and straighten the humble porch.
As he reached out for Ginger's bridle,
he offered his hand to help her dismount,
which he knew perfectly well
she did not need.

She took it awkwardly
and swung down to inspect her new digs.
Ma and Dad were driving
the wagon over tomorrow
with her few things.
Jim thought she'd like
to see the house or the garden,
but she went with him to the barn instead.
He whistled beside her.

The Babymaker

Fantastical testicle
Eject a worm
Whose tantamount mission
Is to squim and to squirm

Thrust through a tunnel
Thrown through a funnel
Threatened by the tomb
Thrashing through the womb

Purposely plowing ahead
To penetrate the prize
Ovulation's standing ovation
Packaged in the monthly surprise

Surviving all obstetrical obstacles
Reviving with virile vigor
Thriving in the fallopian utopia
Arriving where mini-mans are makered

At last we meet, Mon Cherie!
In this bloody improbable back alley
May I open the door for you?
Never mind, I'll bore right through

Wedding granted, soul implanted
Histories colliding, egg dividing
Genetics coding, cells exploding
Impregnated hope, foiled misanthrope

As we leisurely munch on our post-coital lunch
Do we happen to acknowledge
That God just makered a fledgling
Whom we must put through college?

Parents propose to reproduce
But only positively prove the point
The Mysterious Mini-Man Maker
Must choose to anoint

What will have no end
Now has a beginning
One human mended
As the world keeps spinning

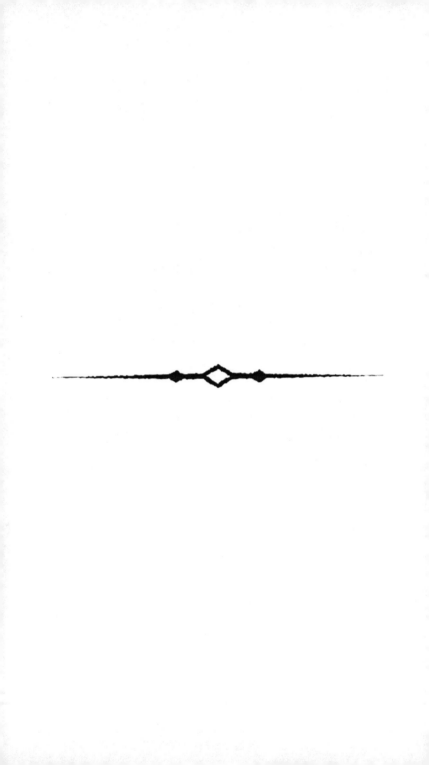

Birth Announcement

Little temple
Little closet for the soul
Landing with a Spirit's breath
Cast upon earth's shoal

Innocent crybaby
Most able to know praise
Because you feast at mama's breast
Left to drift off on her gaze

Leaking lover
A Sabbath rest held in your nap
An umbilical cord stretched from Zion
So you can sit on Daddy's lap

Destined sinner
Free from sinning
Baptized with
A new beginning

Unfolding from your
Little temple
Little closet for the soul

I am from yesterday most recently,
but one hundred days ago many times,
I am from my mama's womb.

I am from my dad's amorous designs,
which are foggy, dubious and
somewhat painful for me to contemplate,
especially since he's here no more.

I am from a prairie ghost town homestead
built by unfortunate, but strengthy arms
who defied the wind with dirt bricks.

I am from a Dust Bowl baby who hated
his one-room-schoolhouse doldrums
but still could quote his Chaucer.

I am from a tiny beauty who taught me
how to set a hospitable table
and do the work that's taken for granted.

I am from a teenage pregnancy all right and tight.
The wedding took place over the state line
because she was too young at home.

I am from this union's one-legged mechanic
who taught me the word *nostril* while
sitting on a sticky, orange vinyl couch.

I am from the stench
of a 4:00 a.m. dairy barn
and a 4:00 p.m. whiskey.

I am from the green fatigues who heard death
on the Philippine front and asked me to trim
his toenails so he could tell me he loved me, once.

I am from blue eyes who deftly decapitated
rattlesnakes with a hoe in the apron
which had baked miles of fragrant white bread.

I am from a Saturday night dance
where an over-the-moon homebody
met post-war Catholic resilience.

I am from this union's milkmaid,
cake-bake seamstress
who sewed her own wedding dress
and then sewed mine.

I am from unspoken love and loss
but never laziness or lack of duty.

I am from hard work,
making something out of nothing—
creativity at its most graceful.

I am from these people, these places.
I shoulder their yesterdays as part of my own.
They teach me where I am going.

Why do I need to write this history, even if most of it turns out to be false: because of the squeaky gleam in my daughter's eye. She peeked at me in the middle of one of her animated dissertations at the breakfast table, and the need to tell her all of this clunked in my stomach. She has to know.

Fear is a sneaky, crackling bitch, mostly because fear shows up uninvited when your pants are inconveniently down. She shows up when I think I'm going to distill hope from my ancestors' stories, but warps my musings into despair instead. I don't want to hand that to my descendants, to my daughter.

For example, how do you grope hope from Mary Isabel Wagner Jefferis' life story? This Ohio native was married at the ripe age of eighteen to Alban Levis Jefferis in 1864, an inauspicious time in our country's history to embark on a new life together. Alban Levis dug ginseng and other medicinal roots to supplement income, and Mary had the honor, nay, the privilege, to begin birthing the first of their ten offspring: nine boys and one girl, the fifth of them being my great-great-grandfather.

Their oldest son, James, died in a hunting accident at the age of fifteen, just as his mother gave birth to her seventh son, George, in 1880. Their sixth son, Charles, died in 1883 at the age of seven, and, unfortunately, George died only five years later at the age of eight, both of unknown causes. Alban Levis then passed away at the age of 53 in 1892, leaving Mary a 46-year-old widow with a three-year-old, seven-year-old and nine-year-old to raise alone. Sometime later Mary's youngest son, Lawrence, was so severely mangled in a hunting accident that Mary had to finish sawing his arm off with a knife. Her brother saw the squalid conditions she and her remaining children were living in and mercifully bought her a milk cow. You're welcome. Mary Jefferis died in Ohio in 1920 at the age of 73.

Did Mary slap her brother for condescendingly giving her more work to do or fall at his feet for his proffered salvation? Did she stare blankly at a cold chink in the wall on the night she buried her firstborn son and nursed her newborn son with her used, tired breasts? Did Mary settle into death comfortably, already well-acquainted, after the deaths of so many familiar to her? I have no way of knowing, but her story has to be told because it holds truth about how to live. Thank you, Grandmother Mary.

Do we come away from her story with hope (*if Mary can live through that, then I can suffer through this lukewarm double mocha latte*) or despair (*life has always sucked the marrow from our bones, from great-grandmother sawing off her son's arm to this darn-it-to-heck lukewarm double mocha latte*)? Do your own emotional homework while I get a box of tissues. My husband thinks the family was not very competent hunters. He does not need to share my tissues.

Perhaps our bourgeoisie lifestyles, fluff-filled with designer coffees, sedate our consciousness from the fact that our lives, as much as they are executed differently, are susceptible to the same vagaries, fears, and horrors that our predecessors faced. The circumstances have shifted from aboriginal hunting accidents to school shootings, but—from the comfort of my automatic leather recliner—I fear for my children just the same.

My children's lives will be fundamentally different, technologically and culturally, from all their ancestors', including mine. I have no history or tradition to glean, no generational wisdom to impart to my children regarding social media or drone deliveries.

But the sterner stuff of life is still to be found in these histories, lives, faiths—these forevers built of days. Mary's story will resonate long after cell phones have been implanted into our brains.

I cannot allow fear to prevent Mary's story from being told. That's the answer to the gleam in my daughter's eye. Whether she digests hope or despair from it matters not, because she'll have recourse to both.

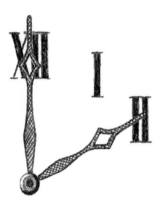

two o'clock

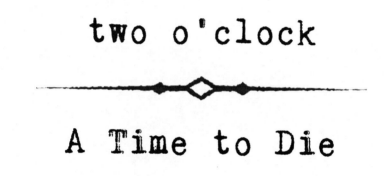

A Time to Die

<u>Time to Go to Time No More</u>

Time slipped, but she didn't see it.

Clock stopped ticking, but he stepped through.

Sun came and went and moon did too.

Happiness followed grief around and stood.

Moment melted, youth faded, old anew.

Weaky-squeaky joints, laugh lines funnel tears.

Time to go to time no more.

Time to go to time no more.

Weaky-squeaky joints, laugh lines funnel tears.

Moment melted, youth faded, old anew.

Happiness followed grief around and stood.

Sun came and went and moon did too.

Clock stopped ticking, but he stepped through.

Time slipped, but she didn't see it.

Cancerous

I remember the pungent fumes of shop grease on your navy work pants. Your back pockets always had a worn ring from your chew.

I remember my first spanking from you with a belt. Bill and I had run in the church.

I remember being jealous of your antacids after every meal—a cooling, peppermint treat!

I remember your side of the bed was the least hospitable for sliding into early in the morning. I always slept on your side after you were gone.

I remember the way Old Spice smelled on you after a shower. It has never smelled the same.

I remember you besting me in a race with your stub and crutches. I couldn't believe I couldn't run faster than you, but your victory did nothing to assure me of your reliability.

I remember the day your hair fell out in the sink. Mom took it harder. The role of comforter fell on you. No leg. No hair. Every time I saw you, there was less of you.

I remember you crutching your way to the bathroom. You didn't make it and puked yellow corn all over the carpet. You apologized to mom as she cleaned it up. I walked away with my heart amputated.

I remember you writhing in pain on all fours in our little apartment in the Bahamas. I could do nothing but disappear.

I remember you watching me in the pool. I was scared to be left alone under your supervision, knowing that neither of us was able to save the other.

I remember you telling me goodbye. Be a good girl for your mama. I love you. I will, Daddy. I love you, too. Bye. I went back to playing on the swing set in the backyard.

I remember praying to you as an angel and then begging God's forgiveness and asking Him to give you a message.

I remember from then on you weren't there; only phantom pains remained.

I remember you weren't there to walk me down the aisle.

The Pillow is Needed

Orange in my memory, black in reality.
"Go get your pillow. He needs it."

"Why would he need a pillow?
I thought you said he was dead."

"Just go get it quickly. They're waiting for you."

I stand there in frozen confusion.
I think it's a little mean to haul away my dad

and take my pillow too.

"Go get it quick!"
I find the pillow in my room,
obeying the word, "Quick!"

I return to the crowded room which parts for me.

My fingers become clammy,
digging in to the tangibility of the pillow,
grasping for an inkling of God.

Eyes attach to me.
A hand extends in expectation.

Why do they want my pillow?

Pillows provide comfort.
The pillow is needed.

Someone expects me to give up my pillow.

"Will I get it back?"
"No, Honey. Daddy needs it."

I mount all my courage
to do the expected thing.

My audience will be so proud.

I hand over the pillow
and watch it suffocate in the melee.

The crowd's attention falls off of me

the instant the pillow leaves my little hands.
The doors close on the ambulance.
My dad and pillow pull away.

I don't feel proud like I thought I would.

I walk back through the kitchen.
I can tell time now. It's 2:00 on April 22, 1982.
That's a lot of twos.

I go back to my room, quick,
to see if my pillow's really missing.

My pillow is gone.

Pillows provide comfort.
The pillow is needed.

The fetid reek of youth lost early.
Front row seat wedged between
more experienced mourners—adults.
My red dress should be black.
Not enough attention.
I am orphan; Mother is widow.
Everyone is here in the gym.
Stupid songs! What is a pall bearer?

Leave my dad alone! He's mine!
I am overlooked,
passed over in favor of
more accomplished mourners—adults,
or pinned condescendingly
with tissue-dabbed glances.

I need a moment alone with him.
I take my place beside
his cold, empty body.

"SPEAK! MOVE! WARM! REACH! SMILE!"

I must perform these simple pleasures for us.
In a covert, sneaked, breath-held moment,
I lift his closed eyelid
and wist for focus of vacant eye.

Someone swats my hand, "No! No!"
I am pulled away.
Dad is taken to a hole in the ground.
I am told to go and play.

31

What I mean by the stench of carnations
is that they flower the dead.
A plastic, unyielding bloom
mirrors the rigor mortis
of what lies beneath.

The carnation intrudes upon
a sultry boudoir of loss and tears,
claustrophobic with blank stares and muddy eyes.

The mourners' senses are already on overload
and threatening to shut down,
when a carnation has the audacity
to assault their sense of smell.

They bring the nose into play
when it's already consumed with breathing.

The carnation stinks up the eye as well,
coming in puckered with
ungodly spray tans of revolting colors.

The stench of the carnation
follows the hearse into the cemetery.
It drools limply over the fresh cut stone
in a fading testimony to loss.
It reminds us that beauty turns to dust,
boasting of life where there is none.

Yet we tolerate the carnation.
We tell ourselves it means well,
while choking on our emptiness.
We voice that the carnation giver
must love us or the dead very much
while we plan revenge on them,
whom were clench-fisted enough
to buy the insult of a carnation.

As if the loss was only worth so much.

Every time you smell them,
even years later,
you will be transported back,
left in the wake
of the same, suffering spot.

Dear mourner,
avoid the carnation.

Griever, Daughter of Leaver

Bye, Dad.
I'm kinda mad at you.
I know it wasn't your fault to leave, but maybe
a little part was your fault,
and I didn't like the way
you left,
so I'm a little mad at you
and a little disappointed, too.

YOU WERE SUPPOSED TO BE PROTECTING ME
when Grandpa was guilt trip perfecting me,
when Mom was tired of neglecting me,
when I was busy deflecting responsibility
off your two other unsuspecting progeny,
when I was projecting my Sunday best
in our white-washed, dysfunctional family.

You were supposed to give me a better ring
than the crap one I got when I turned sixteen.
Was that it?
That was all you had to give me?

Wow.

All these years later,
the pain is scabbed,
decrepit and stale,
side-stepped so long,
moldy and pale.

I'm twelve years older now
than you were when you left,
so I have the straddling
sensation of not knowing
if I'm your parent or the child bereft.

As a parent I want to beat your ass.
As a child I want to turn into your clasp.
As a griever I perceive both options past.

Hello, my name is
Griever, daughter of Leaver,
party of one.
I'm late to the funeral party.
I just found my invitation
to the festivities long ago done.

I guess I'll stay anyway.
Tomorrow's
pathetic heartbreak

will feel better than
today's
faceless heartache.

How to Mother Your Children If Their Father Dies: An Inconvenient 12-Step Program

I'm sorry you need this information. Let's begin because you have to.

1. First of all, you never in a million years thought you would have to navigate this ... shall we say "inconvenience." You signed up for dual parenting when he so thoughtfully provided sperm, and you wound up with a dream come true in your belly. Now you have a nightmare on your hands, and you're alone. Sit with this in sackcloth and ashes. Do not skip this step.

2. Make special sackcloth garments for your children, maybe out of his old t-shirts. Tell them it is their new grieving wear. It works for day and night and is extremely inconvenient, uncomfortable and ugly. They will see you wearing yours and want to be like you. Again, an inconvenience.

3. Provide ashes for everyone by burning up how you thought life was going to be. Allow children to donate to the cause and heap their own ashes on their heads.

4. Take time for nothing. You are going to need a lot of time for nothing because that's all you're going to be able to do effectively. Don't throw yourself into work to sidestep grief and leave your children to fend for themselves.

5. Hold each child alone and individually. Hold your children collectively, as a mother hen with all her chicks. When holding them, explain the dichotomy that everything is OK and that everything is completely destroyed.

6. Cry all the time alone in your bathroom. When your children hear you and say through the bathroom door, "Mama, are you OK?" respond with, "I feel like crying right now." Remember grief must be modeled. Allow your children to do the same.

7. Make a list of twenty people's phone numbers you and your kids can call at any moment, night or day, to talk, cry and/or come over.

8. Talk about your spouse. Do not pretend that pretending he didn't exist will make it easier for anyone. Celebrate his birthday every year as a memorial of gratefulness.

9. Inventory with the kids what they lost when they lost their dad so you know what to mourn. Remember they lost different things than you did when you lost the same person. Remember they lost part of you, too.

10. Give each of the children something that was very special to their dad: something he hand-made, a letter he wrote, jewelry, his Bible or a book he loved, pictures, or his tools. Try not to be selfish, but also keep things for yourself.

11. Say Jesus' name as often as necessary. Talk about your hope, and think of how temporary your separation will really be. Don't put your or your children's faith on trial. Trust it is enough.

12. Smile by inches. Do not be afraid or feel guilty to live. Do not be put off by setbacks in healing. Do not strive for "back to normal." It is a false god.

Wherever you are in this process, God be with you. You may need to visit each step several times. I love you and am sorry for your loss.

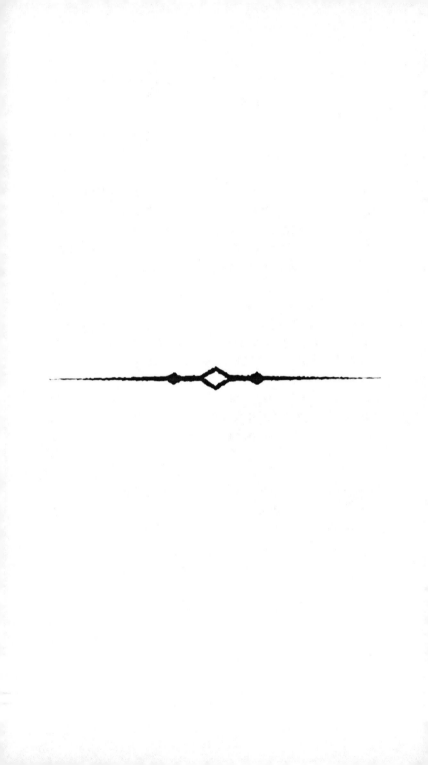

Gone

my fingers are always bleeding
bleeding in memorial to a loss
a loss that requires blood atonement
atonement for what went wrong
what went wrong was that i lost my dad
i lost my dad so the pain vents through my fingers
my fingers are always bleeding

my smile is always leaning
leaning because the world's not quite
not quite straight or whole
whole person went missing
missing someone to turn up both ends
ends of my smile
my smile is always leaning

my sense of time is always fleeting
fleeting years shadow long days
days are long but the years are short
short of childhood crisply lived
lived instead at a rocket's pace to replace
replace the adult i am before i lose my sense
my sense of time is always fleeting

my dad is always gone
gone on to better things
better things than me
me sitting here with bleeding fingers
bleeding fingers and a leaning smile
a leaning smile and a fleeting sense of time
time my dad is always gone

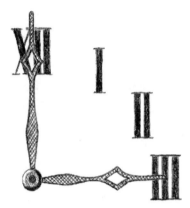

three o'clock

A Time to Plant

Looming Storm

Our heads were down,
bent down,
focused on the busted plow,
our backs bent over Adam's curse.

No one had taken a moment
to notice our environment until
the air shifted, and
we felt the barometer plummet.

Our four heads looked up together.
We took in the dust veil on the horizon
overshadowed by a sickly-green cloud.

Between us and the storm,
our home place was still visible,
a quivering, yet paralyzed rat
on the verge of being snatched by the
rattlesnake storm above it.

We registered the call to action
as well as the lily-livered instinct
to run in the opposite direction.
We girls looked to Grandpa for orders,
but Bill had already begun pitching tools
into the back of the pickup.

Grandpa yelled, "Get in the pickup!"
just as the wind hit and threw dirt in our faces.
Hannah jerked open the cab door
but almost had her shoulder ripped out
as the wind forced past us,
carrying the door as a sail.

We crowded into the cab
with cold-sweat anticipation.
Grandpa brought the '76 Ford to life.
We made a very small dust cloud of our own
as we sprang through the field
headed toward the house to meet the storm.

My Inheritance

I got all of your strength
but was allowed no weakness,
which is a real shame, considering
strength is only found in weakness,

so now I have neither.

I am neither bending with strength
nor broken in weakness.

I have neither the achievements of stamina
nor the missed opportunities of ineptitude.

I have neither the bolster of triumph
nor the bravery of failure.

These all should have been mine to hold and own,
but they were not my inheritance.

Instead I have denial and anxiety,
costly free stand-ins bequeathed in their place:

Denial that the truth happened and
that I was a wide-eyed sparrow caught in its net;

Anxiety that my clipped wings were not imagined.

I accept the net—a little strength to hold.
I know I am afraid to fly—a little weakness owned.

My grace
is enough;
it's all
you need.
My strength
comes into
its own
in your
weakness.

2 Cor. 12:9
The Message

"Man, I wish I wasn't missing recess," she thought as she walked up the hall alone. She was secretly a little proud to be called out for misbehaving, if shoving peas up your nose for cafeteria entertainment could really be classified as bad behavior. It was attention, and personal attention was in short supply.

Mrs. Oblivious had caught her mid-nasal-pea-rocket and asked her to come by her classroom during lunch recess. Being caught was mildly embarrassing, but her academic merits and goody-two-shoes reputation massaged away any misgivings she had about receiving any serious consequences on her way down the hall.

Arriving at her commissioned destination, she knocked on the door. Mrs. Oblivious emerged, closing the door behind her, making up for her height deficiency by crossing her arms forebodingly. "What was that all about in the cafeteria?"

She was thrown off by direct questioning. She had assumed Mrs. Oblivious would immediately launch into a wordy lecture which would only require well-timed nodding.

"Seriously, what do you have to say for yourself? That's not like you."

Somehow, this question released a frenzy of competing thoughts and emotions. She didn't have time, exposed to interrogation as she was in this hall, to weigh out their merits. The defensive responses rose best to the occasion. She blurted, "I think it's because my dad died!"

It sounded absurd to her even as it left her mouth, and yet what slipped was the truest thing she could have said.

Mrs. Oblivious thought it sounded absurd too and despised her confession as a cliché excuse. "What a bunch of baloney. That was five years ago. You can't hide behind that excuse forever!"

Nothing could have hurt her more than her bald confession held in contempt, other than maybe realizing her reality was contemptable and unavailable as an "excuse." She promised Mrs. Oblivious to abstain from all further pea-related activities and promised herself to abstain from baring the truth about her father's memory as she walked back down the hall.

She met the kids, coming in from the recess she had missed, as they chanted, "Pea-brain! Pea-brain!"

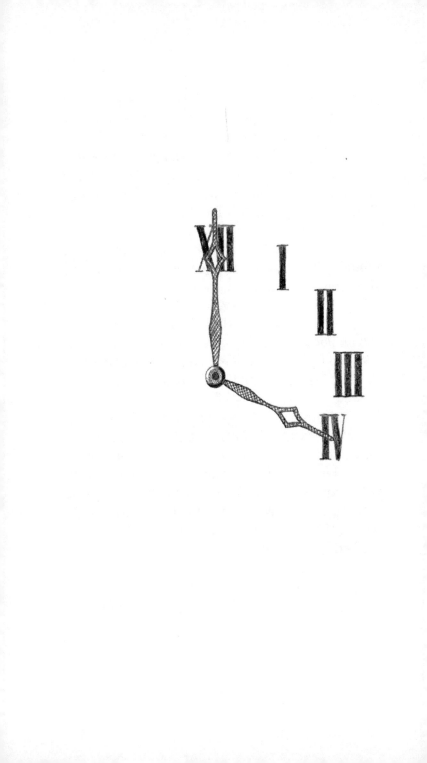

four o'clock

A Time to Uproot

My trophy stood
on my mother's dresser
in her room, not my own.

It was hideously large,
applauding an accomplishment
I no longer celebrated,
but my mother did.

She begged me to take it with me.
In so doing she hoped
I would recognize my achievement
as her own.

I stared at it indecisively.
The inanimate trophy morphed
on the dresser
into a pathetic idol,
its dull plastic golden sheen
reflecting my mother's profile,
warping it toward mine.

She didn't really want it.
She didn't really want me to have it.
What she really didn't want
was for the past to be over
and to be left
with nothing but the trophy.

Leaver, Daughter of Griever

Hi, Mom.
I've been missing you.

I read my journal last night
from my trip to Europe.
That trip was my bridge
from child-woman to woman-child.
When I left it was no secret
I was getting as far away as fast as I could.
I'd done my best, and it was getting no better.

I was struck by how many times I wrote,
"I can't wait to tell Mama,"
or,
"I wish Mama could see this."

We had such a great talk the other day.
At least, I thought so.
You might disagree because
we spent the whole time crying.

Before that, I'd been having such a hard time
reconciling the person who had
unintentionally, yet very effectively
hurt me as a child
with the selfless woman
who spent a month at my house
catering to my every whim
in order to encourage and heal me.

Are you the same person?
Tell me who you are.
I'd like to know since I'm just like you.

I couldn't wait for you to join me
in London all those years ago.
When we were finally united,
you annoyed the hell out of me.
I guess because I could finally let my
exhausted guard down, and
you would still love me.

I don't know what you suffered
when he departed
or when I left.

Forgive me.
Please forgive yourself.
Leavers can return.
Grievers can be healed.

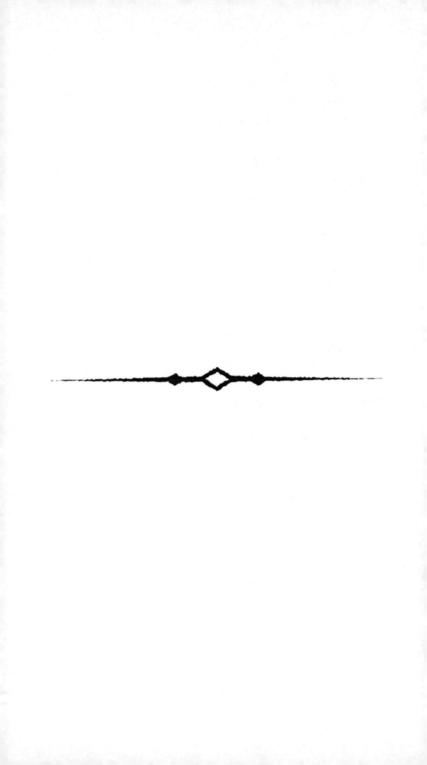

This Is Just to Say
After William Carlos Williams

Dedicated to old loves
who were very good, worthy people,
treated poorly and hurt
by another very good, worthy person

I have bruised
your heart
that was in
my possession

And which
you were unfortunately
entrusting to me

Forgive me
I knew not
what I did
to you

Leaving Tennessee

"There's a time for departure, even
when there's no certain place to go."
Tennessee Williams

Leaving is easy
when you know
where you're going,
Even easier
when you know
you like the place
to which you're going.
I know neither.

I'm not ready.

Time is only distance,
so the time to go is
only to move from here to there.
Distance is bringing unfamiliarity,
which is bringing a decided lack of control,
which is bringing fear so, screw it!

I'm not moving!

While I stay sulking on this obsidian of obstinacy,
the earth spins,
and I know I'm going with it backward.

Backward means coward.

I don't have a certain place I want to go anymore.
I only have a certain person I want to be.
I only want a certain travel companion:

You.

So if You lead at a snail's pace,
then I will lift my weary soul
off this bedrock of backward resolution
and accept that it is

Time to leave.

Take my hand and lead on;
Drag me past my fears.
Just don't expect me to be competent.

When I don't know where I'm going,

It's called faith.

And I only have a mustard seed.

Power Struggle

I wish this box would open.
Implode!
My rage is too impotent,
my angst stymied by my ineptitude.
Therefore all my fictitious audience sees is me
passive aggressively clawing the clear-taped box.
My frustration mounts.
Only dry-heaved tears shed light on my feelings.
The box mocks me.

I look for the damn scissors to inflict
my stifled violence on the tape.
Where are the damn scissors?
Why are the tape and the damn scissors
always conspiring against me?
I will find a knife.

Knife gouges meager hole which is maddening.
I hit the box and resort to
pulling on the tape again with my bare hands.
Is this tape or
tape haunted with a spirit of its own?
It won't rip or release.

I drop the knife, and it skitters on the tile,
able to make the clanging sound I am not.
Do we even need what lies within this horrid box?
I doubt it.

I am exhausted.

I am so weak but no one knows
except box, tape, and knife.
They probably told the damn scissors.

I retrieve the knife and sit down by the box.
I watch my flaccid rage seep back into depression.
I am glad I am alone.
I am so afraid to be alone.
This box! I can't deal with this one box!

Knife in hand,
I slowly stab the tape on one end and cut through.
This mild success uses me up.
I pull the loose end of the tape
released by the knife.
It pulls hard and brings only the reward
of a latent scream.

The far end is still held closed
and defies me still.
I don't want to touch the tape,
so I pretend I don't notice it and
pull the box flaps in opposition.

The bungled tape pops.
The box breaks open.
I fall backward, brutalized on the ground
beside the box, beside the knife.

The box is open, and I am empty.

five o'clock

A Time to Break Down

<u>Twitchy</u>

I'm bored, and I feel twitchy.

Everyone is sick and tired of being sick and tired.

The bed's not made.

The laundry has rotted again
in the washing machine while a huge pile mounts
up in front of it for the same treatment.

The girls are gone,
Pannell is checked out in the bath,
Jude is hogging the TV,
and I just prostituted myself
to the idol of a stupid computer word game.

I missed church today—all of us did.

My head was splitting last night.
More than the ache, it messed with my mind,
that part that feels and sometimes thinks.

I haven't prayed today.

I feel age creeping up on me,
a whispered reality that's already happened
that I just don't know about yet.

I'm scared.

It's not that I wanted more;
I have all that I want.
It's not that I have profound regrets;
I've done the best I've known to do.

It's a malaise,
a discontent that shifts on your thoughts
and shivers along your spine if you sit too long.
It's a disappointment, knowing that this is it,
and the suspicion that you will answer for it.

I've felt hints of more—
more meaning, more fulfillment,
but it's a shadowy,
sand-through-your-fingers sensation.

I feel like crying,
but no one would notice.
If they did,
they would be bored with my tears, too.

O GOD, please help.
I renounce my idols
and throw myself on Your mercy.
I look to You to give me strength and meaning.
Please come to my rescue.
I am not enough on my own.
Isn't that why You named Yourself I AM?
Because You are enough on Your own.

Enough for me.

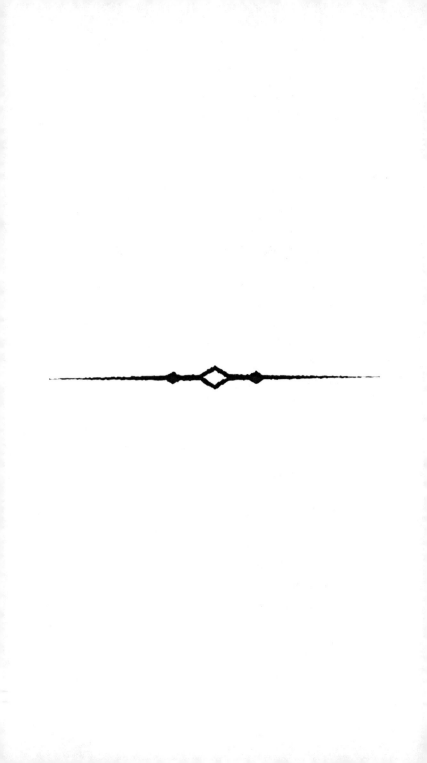

On the Eve of Something Goes Wrong

The poverty of this night lies in the fact that I probably won't be able to remember it.

Haddie's snaggle-toothless grin with her braided bun and adorable buns in skinny jeans.

Merrick rattling off her eleven Bible Busters memory verses, complaining about how much her legs hurt because she leap-frogged around the school track with a friend at recess.

Jude still in his junior high basketball uniform after his game with a fresh haircut, telling me he made the geography bee.

Making Christmas lists, watching Survivor, getting ready for bed, cajoling each one to brush their teeth.

Jude on a beanbag.

Haddie jumping on the end of the couch.

Merrick kissing my forehead as she walks by my chair.

I slid into being anxious.

I drove and contorted
my grief demands
into anxiety.

"Perhaps
Something Terrible
will happen to me."

Rather than accept
Something Terrible
did happen to me.

Anxiety is easier
and less beneficial
than grief.

It allows you to pretend.

I made a mistake.

Anxious, Anxious

I've been spared so much,
but can handle so little.
What I've not been spared is
an anaconda around my middle.
Hope sustains me while my courage fails,
brightness siphoned out through eye sweat trails.
Salty, shiny, wet and briny,
unopposed anxiety knows no propriety.

Patient endurance,
waiting for life to resume
without the glare of despair
and blood-sucking gloom.
"How are you today?"
"I don't understand."
My stomach's in knots
while it's burned with a brand.

My head may explode
from the unretiring electrical misfiring.
I'm asking my heart to beat
while it's broken and crushed.
I know I'm asking of my heart too much.

My limbs are numb, spared from feeling.
My lips are dumb, barren of meaning.
Jaw clenches
on frayed nerve that pinches.

Sunrise, sunset.
Sleepless nights in which my fears
arise, unmet.

Anxious, anxious,
tremble, dissemble

Wait for me on the corner
of Comforter and Mourner.

I'm a successful failure on both streets.

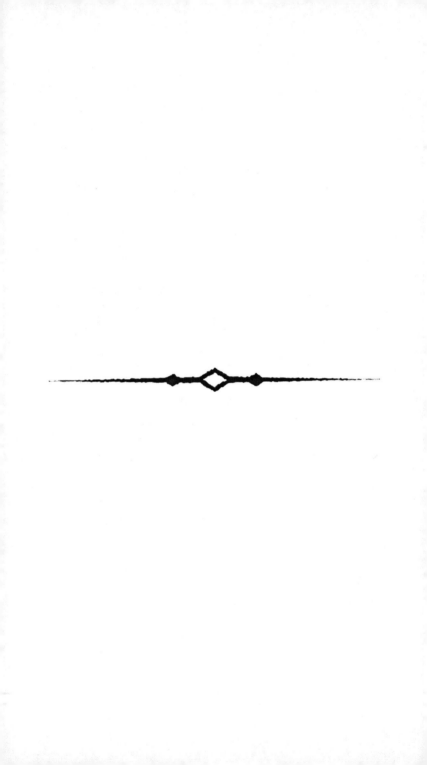

i am so scared this sucks so much i am angry and frightened and i want to protect my baby girl i hate watching her play not knowing how to be thankful for today instead of scared for her tomorrow why cant everything just be normal what the hell is normal why should my baby have to go through this i want to help her what if its the worst what should i do then what if i forget how to take care of her and become a little sticky spot on the pavement of no use to anyone im sick of being the victims people probably dont answer if they see us call its the pannells with another sob story

AAAAAAAAAAAAAAAAAAAAAAAhhhhhhhhhhh!!
Groan.   Weight. Burden.
Spider webs. Dense undergrowth.

In this vast, vast universe
where God is God,
what are my options?
God, be with us.
Please don't leave our side.
Walk with us step by step.
Open up doors of understanding and possibility.
Help us to submit to what you are doing with us.

HELP! HELP! HELP!

Tonight Is Just a Night

Tonight is a really hard night.
Tonight is a really hard night.
I am very scared and alone.
I wonder how this will get better.
I wish for other circumstances.

Devious thoughts flit
uncontrolled around my mind.
I hear through the grapevine that it's my job
to trap and tame these sneaky, slippery bastards.
That seems laughable.

I'm so tired.
I have only the energy to lie in bed
and notice the static bursts of
negative energy in my head.

Haddie's not seeing well and has to have an MRI,
adding to our high anxiety level.
Pannell hit a horse and
totaled our truck on Thursday.
Thank God he's fine.
No word on the horse.
Genevieve is dying.
Merrick had her first panic attack tonight,
complete with hyperventilating.

I hope you have no idea what it's like
to talk your ten-year-old baby girl
through an anxiety attack,
finally get her to sleep,
and then have one of your own.

God is on His throne, and He hasn't forgotten me.
Lord, have mercy on me, a sinner.
Into Your hands I commit my spirit.
The LORD is near to my broken heart.
I will cast my burdens on Him for He cares for me.

With all the strength that God gives me,
I write, "Tonight is just a night."
Tonight is just a night.
However badly it sucks, I will get through it.
Healing is a process, not an overnight campaign.
Patient endurance is my right hand.

To All the What Ifs I've Loved Before

We're breaking up.
I should have quit you sooner.
You're a tragic lover.

We spent too much time
on the cold couch of idle imaginings
instead of snuggled together
with lucid logic.

Remember that time when you said,
"What if Pannell dies?"

You inhaled so much gratification
from seeing me twisted.
I was messed up for days.

"What if you can't pay your bills?"
"What if they don't like you?"
"What if Hadassah has a brain tumor?"
"What if you go to hell?"

Well,
if I do,
I'd be there with you
saying,

"What if we had broken up sooner?"

Me and Jesus Dialogue

Me: Jesus, I'm so sorry, but I couldn't have been your mom. (With feeling, choking on a sob)

Jesus: I know, you idiot. That's why Mary was.

Me: (With sangfroid) Well, I'm glad we got that out of the way. I felt like I had to confess it. I can't stand the world's pain, and I couldn't have witnessed Yours like she had to.

Jesus: It's over now. It is finished. I won.

Me: I know. That's what You've told us, but did You really win? Why isn't this craphole less crappy?

Jesus: Because you have to poop. What goes in must come out or you'd get very sick.

Me: OK ... (Pausing, not knowing what to say, and then ...) Are You really here with me? I positively have to know again today. I know You were yesterday, but today seems different, and I can't seem to hold on to what I knew for certain yesterday.

Jesus: Turn around. Do you see Me?

Me: (Turning around expectantly, then spinning back around, disappointed and furious) NO! I don't see You! Stop playing games with me. I'm so fragile and weak.

Jesus: I asked you to look, and you obeyed because you already know I'm here with you. So believe with all that part of your heart that made you look over your shoulder that I will *never, ever* leave you alone.

Me: But what if You plus me is not enough? You know I'm less than a worm.

Jesus: I really wish you weren't so stupid, Darling.

Me: *So do I!* You're the One that made me like this, so don't blame all my stupidity on *me*! (Huff, huff!)

Jesus: Why don't you just cry with Me for a while?

Me: I'm sick to death of crying. In fact, I want to scream my head off, but I've lost my sound. My soul has squeezed it shut.

Jesus: I know what that feels like—dumb!

Me: I suppose You do. It sucks, right? What about this part of my heart that feels like it's been beaten with a baseball bat and then shredded with a grater? I suppose You're going to tell me You know what that feels like, too.

Jesus: Yes, I remember what that feels like, but I just kept seeing your beautiful face.

Me: That's the stupidest thing I've ever heard. If my heart is an ugly customer, my face is worse.

Jesus: You don't even know your real name yet. How could you possibly judge what you look like to Me?

Me: Well, I can't, but I've seen glimpses.

Jesus: Weren't the glimpses beautiful?

Me: Yes, they were, but so fleeting and so different from the mirror that I can't comprehend if they are real or not.

Jesus: They are real, and everything else is not. There is so much Good in the world. Hold on. I am making all things new.

Me: Could You please hurry?

Jesus: I'm on it, but today is just Me and you.

Me: OK. I really want that. Do You know I love you?

Jesus: When did I win you over? Was it My stunning creation? My sacrifice? My witty Sermon on the Mount?

Me: I love Your creation, even though I take it for granted too often. I don't know what to do with Your sacrifice; You're like that annoying friend who gives me a $100 gift card for Christmas when all I got them was a hastily scribbled Dollar Store card. And frankly, Your Sermon on the Mount always has me thinking I'd better saw off my arm. I think I love You most when I realize I'm really not a worm to You.

Jesus: Maybe you're not so stupid after all.

Me: See, You made me this way!

<u>Waiting In a Deep Pit At the Back of a Cavern on a Moonless Night</u>

Light always conquers the dark,
but several places exist
that make it hard for light to prevail:
say a deep pit, a cavern, a moonless night.

I found myself
in a deep pit
at the back of a cavern
on a moonless night.
I was afraid and alone.

I never despaired because I knew
you would come for me and find me,
but I had to wait until you came,
and that wait was excruciating.

I waited in the bottom with wordless leeches
that greedily sucked my own words dry.
I waited at the back with nameless, distorted faces
who identity hacked the faces of those I held dear.
I waited on the dark with fears
which made themselves real with false light.
I named my sobs, thankful that I could weep.
I whispered the name of Jesus, and I waited.
My frustration at my owned
and unwanted helplessness mounted,
salting my lacerated feelings.
I waited some more.

I heard you before I saw you
which made no sense because
light is supposed to travel faster than sound.
You were far away, but I recognized your voice.

A small ray of hope
reached the bottom of my pit,
evaporated the word leeches, and I sputtered,
"Help! I'm down here."

You yelled back, "We know, Dummy!
How did you get all the way down there?"
I smiled, and the nameless faces
standing guard over my misery
dissolved into your very real, lovely countenances
secure again in my mind.

Fear holds on the longest.
While I endured your interminable approach,
fear had its way with me.
I was afraid you'd give up
on your own problematic journey to find me
and turn away, freed from the bother of me.
I was afraid you'd put forth your best effort,
but your rope to reach me would be too short.
I was afraid that you would reject me
and leave me in the pit when you saw
my leech emaciated body,
my fear deranged mind, and
my soul on bad credit, unable to give charitably.

Hope is a precursor to light,
and light will always win the day.
My fears did not dictate
your performance on my behalf.

Your faces peeped over the edge of my pit,
and the light you carry in your eyes
reached my rock bottom.
I shivered in my humiliation,
and you smiled for me.

It took a while to get me out of the pit,
a dead weight task.
I hung both my arms
around the necks of your encouragement.
We reached the mouth of the cavern just as
the moonless night gave way
to a drizzly Oregon morning.

We sat down exhausted and punchy.
You were amused by my progress.
I was bemused by
your sincere efforts on my behalf.
We talked about good times we've had together,
carefully tiptoeing around the raw topic
of the most recent past.

I tried to tell you how grateful I was
for your part in my rescue, but you cut me short,
partly in an attempt to downplay
my sense of travailing gratitude,
partly because you didn't want to betray
what you had risked to get to me,
partly because you had no real idea of that
from which you had rescued me.

I held your hands while you prayed,
and then I mumbled toward heaven.
When we were strong enough,
we got up and slowly walked our separate ways.
You kept glancing over your shoulders
to make sure I was steady.

I stood up straight in rebellion
to the nagging predatory fears that followed me
out of the pit
from the back of the cavern
on a moonless night.
They still nipped at my heels
as I stepped on their heads.
I waved to signal you that I was OK.

What makes a shadow?
Something that blocks the light.
What trumps a shadow maker?
A mirror that reflects the light into the shadow.
That's what you've been to me:
a mirror reflecting light into my dark place.

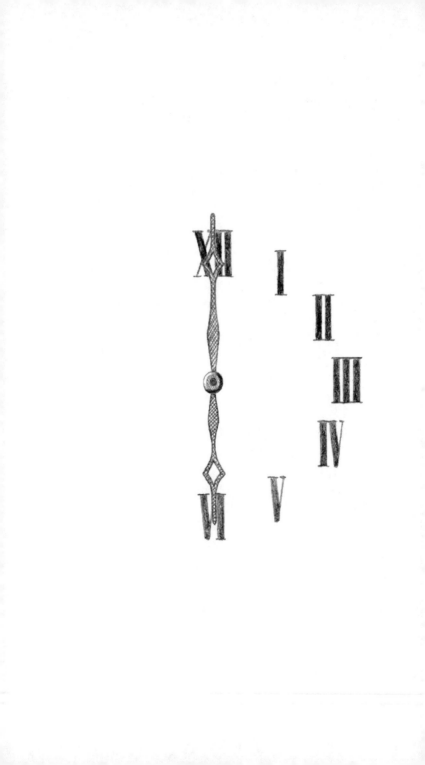

six o'clock

A Time to Heal

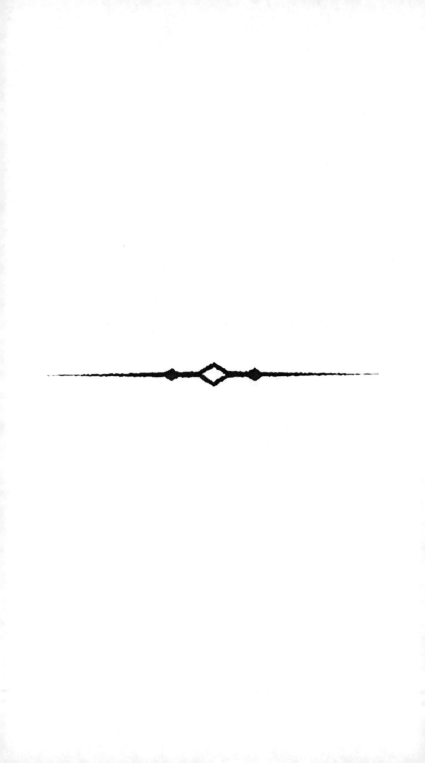

First Date

I'm about to meet with a counselor.

She's late, and I'm early.

How is that to be interpreted?

I brought a notebook,

my checkbook,

and tissues.

I toyed with bringing my Bible

but decided against it.

I'm drinking tea,

a relaxed and casual smokescreen,

all the while

enumerating my exits.

Routinely Resurrected

Quiet sunlight climbing

Through the pane of my window

Fading moonlight kiting

Blue on a skein flying low

Trade-off handshake

A kiss in the dew

Revolving earthquake

Executed without skew

Night has become as far away as can possibly be.

Day has brought this jar of clay new mercy to me.

The Lord's Prayer

Reminded of what you cannot force
and is not to be readily found,
choose to kneel on the cold, hard ground.

Trying again to go to the Source
with an inward shudder, knee pain
closed eyes, bowed brain:

"Maker in Eternity,
I recognize You are sacred.
You forever rule on land and in sky.
Today I need food.
Look past my idiocy, and
I'll try to extend grace
to fellow idiots that annoy or hurt me.
Keep me from being stupid.
Guard me from Hate.
For Yours is the real all day long."

Ease up off the floor.
Is it an altered affair
since you suffered your knees in prayer?

No, but yes.
Reality opened and listed.
For a moment
something shifted.

Me and Leviathan Dialogue

Me: Hello, Leviathan. I met you when I was very young. When I was innocent and ignorant of you, you forced our acquaintance. What do you have to say for yourself, O Fear of Death?

Leviathan: I took on the task to make death a curse, and I have done my job well.

Me: Indeed you have. I must compliment you on your success. I want to ask you when you'll come for me (would that alleviate or intensify my fears?), but I know you're not in charge of the number of my days.

Leviathan: I have never been in charge of death. I am only God's agent, but people's sins are ever before them so they wrongly give me the fear they owe God, which plays nicely into my voracious jaws. My dessert is human anxiety. I suck on it after I crush your windpipe.

I know I will not get to feast on your bones, O Daughter of the Most High God, and you know it too, yet you let me instill you with fear."

Me: You are certainly to be respected, O Curse of the Flesh, but I follow the One who is the Firstborn of those who escape your teeth. He will not let you harm me.

Leviathan: If that is true, why are you afraid? I smell it on you, and it fuels my raging appetite.

Me: Because I know those stronger and braver than me that have fallen prey to your traps. I mourn those you have caught up in your claws.

Leviathan: Ah ... God must have abandoned them to my grave, and so you naturally distrust Him with your own soul. I like where this is going. You begin to tempt me very much, and I see I'm having the same success with you.

Me: True, You Liar, you have had success with me. You have tricked me into misdirecting my fear. I will transfer my fear to the One who deserves it, and not let my fear be an idol's offering I sacrifice to you.
```
'Death has been swallowed up in victory.
Where, O Death, is your victory?
Where, O Death, is your sting?'
```

Leviathan: If you believe that, then what do you want with me, Imperishable? I will go my own way to gorge on more willing victims, but I will not forget you so you had best be tenacious with your beliefs. Until a more opportune time, au revoir.

Me: I cannot fight you, even though I rage at your destruction and lies and malice. I will leave you to be conquered by the Rider on a White Horse.

```
For He must reign until He has put
all His enemies under His feet. The
last enemy to be destroyed is death.
I Corinthians 15:26,55 NIV
```

Today I want to do so many things,

which is different from the days

when I have to do so many things,

which is different from the days

when I have to do so many things

that I don't want to do,

which is different from the days

when the word "do" is inconceivable.

Today I will handpick

from a luscious selection

of things I want to do

and bask in the glory of doing them.

One Day Two Ways

One day

    One day

We will feel well

    We will all die

And have a day of happiness

    And have a day of mourning

All together

    All alone

And the sun will shine

    And the fog will descend

And I will feel skeptical.

    And I will have hope.

101

Authority of Hope

I need a
bird of hope.

In my imaginings
I am wrapped in light:

> goodness, joy, peace,
> > faithfulness, patience
> > > gentleness, kindness,
> > > > control and love.

> > > > The birds come to me
> > > with banners in their beaks.

> > > Noah's dove brings me assurance.
> > Moses' quail brings me abundance.
> Elijah's raven brings me attendance.
God's Spirit brings me abidance.

Each one is given to endow
me with each one of these
qualities, protecting
an authority
of hope.

Finch and Daisy

The finch came in strong and hot,
yet somehow landed so lightly.
Showing off his staying power,
he swayed gently on the decaying daisy stem.
For a moment, the finch took in his surroundings,
and solidly said to himself,
"I am Finch, and I am no other."

Then began the bobbing and weaving,
head-tapping contortions.
He danced with the daisy's shaven head.
They'd danced this dance before, earlier in the fall
when Daisy still had something to give:
the little seeds that Finch loved.
Finch rattled her down to her stalk,
and then reminded himself,
"I am Finch, and I have my dignity."

He changed his tact and used Daisy
only as a contrasting backdrop
to his magnificent plumage.
He lolled his head and darted his eyes
to advertise to nearby admirers
and survey more promising, less desolated daisies.

The air stilled,
a snowflake gasped,
Daisy resigned,
and Finch rejoiced!

He could rest so weighty on that spent daisy
because he knew he could fly.

I watched all this from my window by the door
and tasted the tang of a cleanness beyond myself.
I was reluctant to dethrone Finch
or embarrass Daisy,
but I opened the door and walked through,
joining the space where
they were a world unto themselves.

Finch arrested his preening
and shot off the shuddering daisy.
I heard him beating his wings at me,
"I am Finch, and I am not yours."

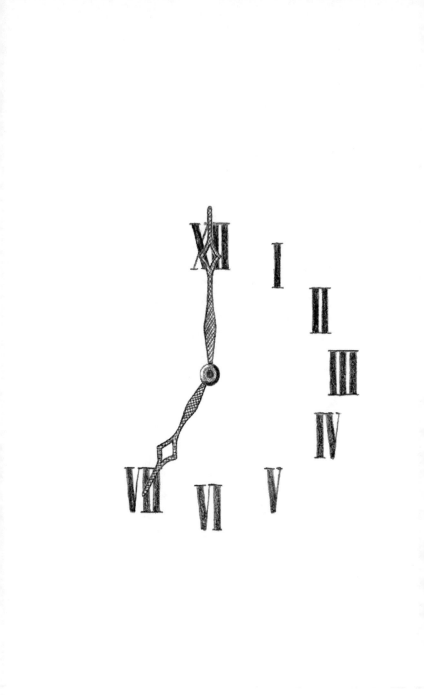

seven o'clock

A Time to Embrace

Why Didn't We Kiss?

Were my vinegar lips too chapped?
Was your cynical heart too cold?
Why didn't you stand under the mistletoe?

Did you discover a fungus among us?
Do you feel a gap mushroom between us?
Does past mistletoe experience grieve us?

Could it be you forgot to pucker and withdrew?
Can you argue that I ran out of luck?   Or were you
Caught playing the field and it caused you to yield?

Have you persistently protested mistletoe death?
How about the minty freshlessness of my breath?
Has kissing become a snoring, boring chore?

Any cold sores and their sources causing concern?
Are you hesitant to swap spit under a bower?
About to be a public-display-of-affection coward?

Is this Christmas tradition too old or too young?
If I were to solemnly swear to no tongue?
I cannot conspire with you to mutual my desire?

Will we never contemplate kissing again?
Who will we be—lovers or just friends?
Why didn't you stand under the mistletoe?

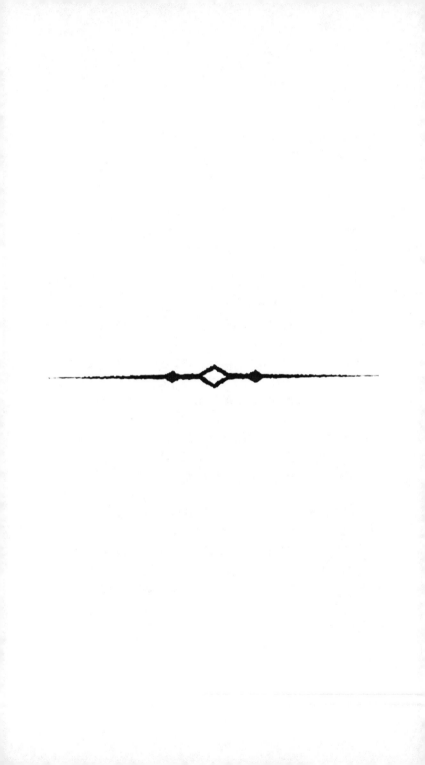

I'll Always Wait

You are gone, and I've lost my footing
on what I know as real and true.
You are coming back but not right now.
I'm under the weather of relational flu.

You are living large in the big city
while I labor with our lives' mundane.
You are rubbing your extrovert shoulders
while my pillow softens the blow of going insane.

You are getting what you want in life.
I'm happy for you,
but I don't seem to get my fair share.
You are sorry for me and wish me very happy.
I want to punch the condescension off your face
or play the martyr in our affair.

You are not here for me to punch your face,

or to hug me,

so I'll wait for you to come home.

We'll be good until life throws another curve ball.

I'll always wait for you to come home.

Could Should Would

I know I am brave and bold,
so I thought that I could
let you go, but I soon
discovered that I couldn't.

I know I wanted you to go,
and I thought that you should,
but when my bravery broke
then I knew that you shouldn't.

I know I usually toughen up,
and we thought that I would,
but my new found sense of worth
demanded that I wouldn't.

Maybe I could have let you go,
but I shouldn't like to know
if I would have had tomorrow
whole or with a powder-burned ego.

<u>You Whole</u>

Everything you give me is

bro
  ken •

Rusted intentions
Busted decisions
Ill-trusted inventions

All hiding behind
And holding back

The one thing you could give me
That I need—

You whole.

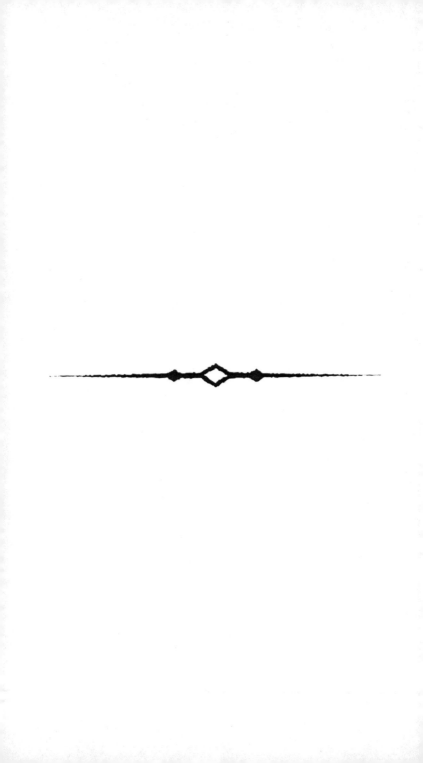

Ho-Hum

When you're falling in love
the intense elation you feel
is not that the one you love
is empirically more exquisite.

It's that in their eyes
you see all at once the condensed promises
of your coming days not spent alone.

At their touch you understand
someone will hold you
on that heinous, bad day.

In your shared kiss
you taste the future
held together in an inside joke.

After you've fallen in love
it's easy to confuse
the diminishing, transient feelings of ecstasy
with something humdrum and ho-hum,
a vanilla answer to your chocolate craving,

when they look into their eyes and laugh,
when they kiss you at the door goodbye,
when they touch your hair
in the same way they've done a thousand times.

The sharp expectancy
has become your day-to-day reality.
Feast on your ho-hum.

Résumé to Stay in Your Life

Objective

To be an integral and indispensable contributor to the marriage team while retaining impressive and attractive attributes of my own individuality.

Education

Sunday School, Flagler, CO
- Foundations in fundamentalism

K-12 in the same building, Flagler, CO
- Third generation

Harding University, Searcy, AR and Florence, Italy
- MRS degree

University of Memphis, Memphis, TN
- Grad school dropout

Doula Certification, Medford, OR
- Mastered stewed placenta recipe

Community QuickBooks class, Medford, OR
- Emphasis on in-the-red accounting

Experience

- Learned to drive and parent by age ten
- Performed well in school: Valedictorian
- Lost dad, grandpas and two children
- Moved cross-country twice to people and places unknown
- 19 years of hard labor as your wife
- 14 years of indentured servitude as the mother of your children

118

Strengths/Weaknesses
(Hard to tell apart)

- Large birthing hips
- A smidge of self-diagnosed general anxiety disorder with a dash of obsessive compulsive behaviors
- Good listener and empathizer
- Nice handwriting—a must in today's world
- Perfectionist with high standards and expectations
- Funny and dearly love to laugh
- I know of God a lot. I know God a little.

Summary

Please consider me for the prestigious position of remaining your wife. My faults are multitude, but I am quite charming, witty and beautiful. You'd be lost, alone, and doing your own laundry and checkbook without me. A worse fate for you I could not imagine.

Regretfully Yours

I regret not writing you a love note
for your suitcase
when you left for
your first grad school class.

At the time, I probably
didn't feel every flowery word
I would have written,
but they were still true.

You deserved it,
and I got lazy.

Here's my negligent, belated
summation of what that regretted
note would have said:

>   My Dearest Nelly Bear,
>
>   I love you a little and a lot.
>   I'm so pleased you're mine.
>   I'm thankful for the life we have.
>   I am not the same when you're gone.
>
>   Regretfully yours,
>   Jess

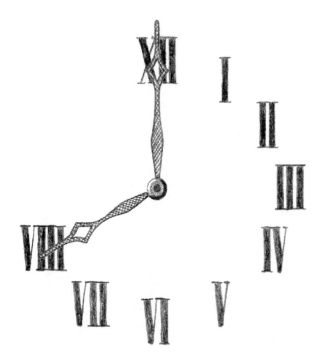

eight o'clock

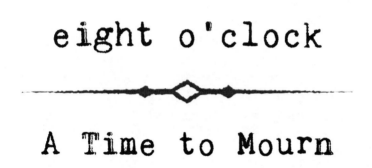

A Time to Mourn

Quitting Codependency

When did I go right when you went left?
It was at the cut of the knife.
The cut was so stunning, so smooth,
we didn't feel it until we saw the blood testify
to the severed bond of Siamese twins.

I'm not sure we ever acknowledged
the choice to separate,
the ability for me to go right
and you to turn left,
until the knife showed us the way
and enlightened us to the painful possibility.

Now we're left alone to know the wound,
clean up the blood
and make decisions on our own.

I blame you for my vulnerability,
although I know it's not a fair liability
to lay at your door.
It wasn't you who initiated my codependency,
and it wasn't you who wielded the knife.
Who was that anyway?
I should remember to care sometime.

I hate the knife, and yet I'm thankful.
It gave us the gift of a precise cleave
instead of a gangrenous tear.
Do you feel the same way, too?

I'm going to walk around the block

`alone`

to see if I can by myself.

If we meet again
after our points of separation have healed,
maybe we could hold hands
but not because we have to.

Cleaning Up After You

One past due conversation
brought it all back,
smashing through my security.

You jimmied open my back door,
dunned my locks,
shattering the glass of my serenity.

I sat there and let you
in frozen, faked grace,
smile plastered in place
on my Picasso'esque face.

You didn't mean to,
innocent of intent.
Why does that necessitate
more torment?
Because I must forgive
the damage you inflicted
and your ignorance.

Now I pace and scuttle,
broom and dustpan in hand,
to tackle the debris,
mumbling to myself
that once upon a time
I had dreamt of being
something more than a janitor
to my shattered resolve.

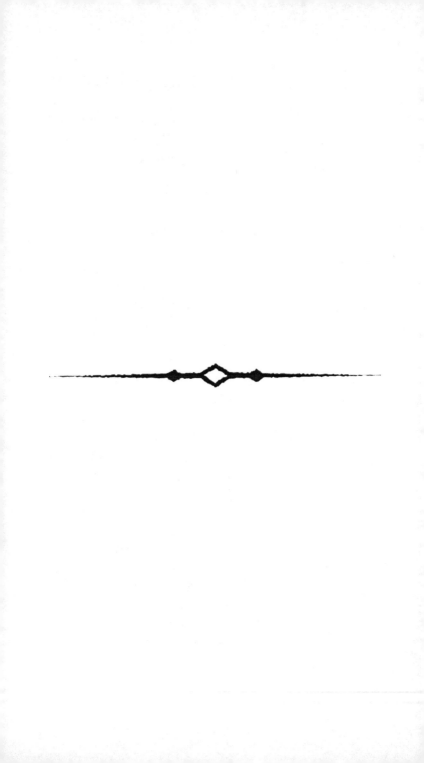

A Pauper's Present

I want to tell you we are going to make it,
but I don't know the future.
I know about the sting
you carry in your eyes.
I recognize the taut jaw
and the saddled shoulders.
I smell what's happened.
I want to spit it out.
I'm wary of your pain,
because I have my own, you know.

I want to tell you we are going to make it
to the denouement.
It's important that you hear me.
Suffering doesn't side-line us
unless we refuse it as a travel companion.
If you take the pain with you,
I'm coming, too.

I don't have a remedy, unless it's that I can
bathe your brow in lavender water,
drink tea in your company,
sing *You Are My Sunshine*,
bake you a cookie,
kiss your temple,
send you a card,
believe.

That's what I've got to get us there:
A pauper's present for a prince among men.

Gallant Genevieve

My favorite people
are those who make you feel like
you are special, even though
they are the heroes.

Take my dear friend, Genevieve, for example.
I wish I could bottle Genevieve
and market her to you as "Essence of ..."
Well, I'm stuck searching for the right word
that could capture her entirely.
You'll have to supply one for me.

Your word will have to encompass
unassuming, gracious, humorous, gentle,
living lightly with great and mighty roots,
sitting with suffering, simple, appreciative,
dutiful, unafraid, and pleasant.

Hero, indeed!

However, with this great litany of attributes
in her back pocket,
in every conversation with her
I came away with her assurance
that *I'm* amazing.

Sometimes I thought she
had an outmoded understanding of amazing:
like I'm amazing because I knew how
to turn on her DVD player, and she did not.

Gen was the best person to show you how to
grow old with your personhood intact,
hope for eternity with a growing faith,
and take each day just as you find it:
not so bad that it doesn't deserve
for you to put on your clip-on earrings.

My shirt still smells like her perfume,
Essence of Gallantry,
from hugging her for perhaps the last time.
When she said goodbye,
her final words to my crying Merrick were,
"You don't be sad about me.
I'm happy to be going.
You just go and live a good life."

With long life I will satisfy *her*
and show *her* my salvation.
Psalm 91:16 NIV

I have loved you very deeply, Gen,
and I am not unaware of the gifts of friendship
you offered to me and my family,
though you thought you had nothing to give.
I will see you soon,
be very glad of your company
and be so honored to meet Clark.

<u>Lost and Never Found</u>

I know you, but I don't know you.

I have your genetics and your smile,
but you're an alien.

I know your shoe size
and the catalogue of your aches and pains,
but not what really hurts.

I know your habits and your medications,
but not why you take them.

I know your timeline,
but no moment can I hold onto and say,
"Aha. I have found you."

I look back to the day we sat on the swing.

You uttered an underbelly whisper,

{Back—and—forth}

{Back—and—forth}

"I never thought I would…"

132

The unfinished phrase stretched tight on the hush.

I leaned in close.

I knew if you finished that sentence in my hearing
at last I would be able to say,
"Aha. I have found you."

We sat on the swing.

{Back—and—forth}

{Back—and—forth}

You never finished that sentence.

P. S. You died later. You were sick, but said you weren't. Do I
have less of you now that you're gone than I did when we rocked
back and forth? I don't think so. You departed from me, and I never
knew you.

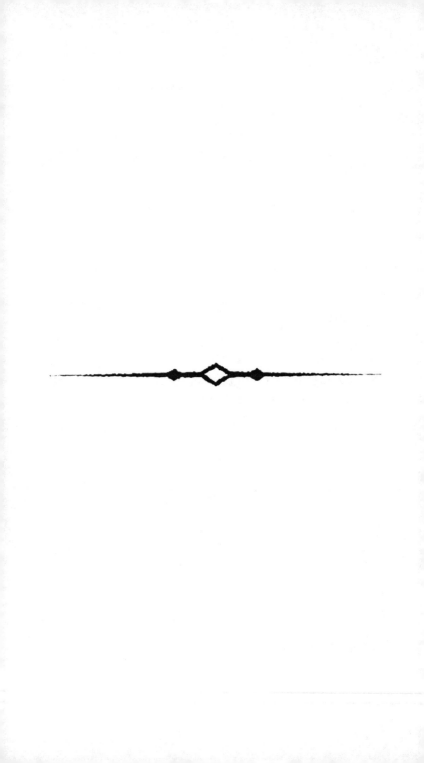

Relief Is in the Pain

Some days don't come candy wrapped.

They fall hard from the sky

and shatter onto the pavement.

You have to walk these days with bare feet.

The danger is inevitable:

you will step on splintered dreams.

When you pull them out,

you will discover the relief is in the pain.

You are never closer to faith

than when you sit beside your doubts.

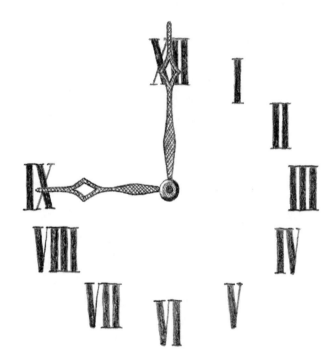

nine o'clock

A Time to Dance

What Happened Today?

What indeed distinguishes today from any other?

Genevieve would remark upon the weather and tell you what they had for dinner and how her sister's health maintains.

Margie would tell you about the owl she saw in the old cottonwood tree at the quarter moon and that she also had a coyote through the yard.

Nelda would hand you a new shoe catalog to peruse while she disparaged presidential candidates for the upcoming elections while checking to see what new British period pieces may be available on DVD.

Dallas would say that aphids have him driving all over Flagler, America checking fields. While out and about, he drove down to see his mom in the nursing home, keeping up a steady diet of cell phone conversations on the way regarding the children's home board meeting until his signal went out at Kit Carson.

Rose would simultaneously bemoan and brag about the littered path of destruction and undisposed food garbage left in the wake of a visit from any number of her ten cherubic grandchildren.

Pannell would say some notable rock legend died today and that the world is spinning void of their particular brand of musical genius. Never mind their drug addictions and crimes against children. It only served to spur their art. Then he would make a playlist in their honor to help the uninitiated to appreciate the fallen.

Jude would reply, "Uh ... nothin'," imperiously jaded by twelve swollen years of disappointed expectations brought to ground by the monotonous blandness of middle school.

Merrick would quest on and on that So-and-So called Whosoever a dork which made her hellfire mad, only she can't say "hellfire," so she made a dimpled mean face instead.

Haddie would proudly inform you that she did nerd math in the hall with other bespectacled children while the rest of the class remained seated in the classroom to endure the mere basics of addition.

I would say that I paid bills and did payroll and fielded well-intentioned inquiries into the status of my emotional health. Then I took a hot bath, grabbed one too many handfuls of chocolate chips, and went to writing class.

I cried the day you were born
   because you were more beautiful
   than I could have ever imagined.

I cried the first Sunday I took you to church.
   We celebrated communion,
   and, for the first time, I had the faintest idea
   of what God gave up when He gave up His Son.

I cried the day I almost dropped you,
   and first failed you as a mother.

I cried the night a bee stung you in your crib,
   and I witnessed you in pain I could not avoid.

I cried when you puked on me at a wedding,
   and then pooped in the bath
   I gave you to wash off the puke.
   You drew all over the kitchen floor with syrup
   while I cleaned the poop out of the tub.
   Needless to say, you needed a bath again.
   I cried in frustration as I cleaned up the syrup
   because you required so much of me.

I cried when you chose Daddy over me,
   and of me you required less.

I cried the day you told me not to walk you
   to your kindergarten classroom anymore.

141

I cried when you gave a slideshow presentation
   of your mission trip work in Mexico.
   You were gone so long and didn't mind.

I cried driving you home
   from your ear surgery at the hospital.
   You could hear me and Daddy
   talking in the front seat, whispering even,
   something you could never have done before.

I cried the day I hung up your clothes
   on adult hangers because, after only seven years,
   your clothes fell off the children's hangers.

I cried when we finished reading Harry Potter.
   We were so full of wonder together,
   lamenting its finale.

I cried when I took you
   for your first day at a new school.
   I felt despicable for leaving you alone
   in a strange place with strange people.
   I walked around and around the track
   outside the school just to be close to you.

I cried when I pulled you out of the van
   by your hair and yelled at you.
I cried more when I apologized
   and you rubbed my back and said it was OK.

I cried when I first heard you cuss.
  I had no idea you weren't perfect.
  I mourned our lost naiveté.

I cried when you made an amazing stop in goal,
  when you missed making the save,
  when you won the spelling bee,
  when you lost the spelling bee.
  You can't imagine my pride.

I cried the day you turned thirteen
  because you were a teenager
  which meant you had a cell phone
  and might get brain cancer
  and disproportionate thumbs
  and forget how to make eye contact
  and form complete sentences.

I cried the day I discovered you had outgrown me.
  I knew myself to be at a disadvantage
  and that you didn't have to listen to me
  unless you chose to.

  I know I have more tears to cry
  because we have a little way to go.
  But on the days you
  graduate, leave, get married, or go to Jesus,
  I'll only need a few tears, because
  for your love, hurts, successes and failures,
I cried along the way.

A Hairy Conversation

I glance over and inwardly gasp. Once again, parenthood has me on my back heels. Merrick is chatting away to me from the passenger seat. In her usual animated fashion, she raises her bare arms to emphasize her point, and I see it:

One long, dastardly pubescent arm pit hair.

The scene is staged, and it is up to me to act on it. How will my words be received? With embarrassment? With tears? With defensiveness? I could ignore it, pretend I didn't see the heralding sprout.

Why do we have armpit hair anyway? How is it in any way necessary to the reproduction process? Ugh! I digress.

Pull it together, Jess. If you don't say something, that little brat boy who teases her about her bra will notice it and mortify her the next time she wears a sleeveless shirt. Mother up, but proceed with caution. If you mess this up, she may be a high school dropout. No pressure!

"So, Merrick, have you ever practiced shaving?" There's no going back. I have pulled the trigger.

"Well, Mama, sometimes when I'm in your shower, I use your razor on my birthmark," with a sheepish, confiding grin.

So far so good, but it doesn't seem as if she intuited where I'm going here. I go for broke, "Well, it looks to me like you might need a razor for something else. You have a little friend in your armpit." I drop the bomb with a smile to try for jocular over derision.

Wait for it ...

"I know, right!! It's so long and cute I want to tie a bow on it. I have more over here, but they're not as long!"

Hmm ... accepted and cultivated, are they? The plot thickens.

"Well, they're quite charming, but what are you going to do about them? Cherish them and go French or shave them?"

"Will it hurt?"

"No, Baby; they will die a merciful death."

I announced I was going on a walk, and you asked if I wanted you to come. I said you didn't have to, secretly trying to play you off for a little time to myself but not such a jerk that I could refuse you outright. You decided to go—for my sake, of course.

We both had to trade in our flip-flops for sneakers. We got to the mailbox before I noticed you had no jacket. Of course, you did not need one because you were already hot, and it was a sultry 55° outside.

You encouraged me to go on ahead because you love to run to catch up. I wogged for all I was worth, but I was no match, and you had me. We joined hands, and you didn't stop talking.

We rounded the corner and came upon the ditch of purple windflowers that only bloom in February. You picked one for each of us, and the sun was exhilarating.

You made me go to the side of the road, close my eyes and bend down so you could "secretly" install my flower between my glasses and my ear. You were a little embarrassed that I indulged you in such child-like behavior.

You told me that you and Merrick have also had excellent conversations on this same walk around our neighborhood. I felt the proud lookupingness you have for your sister, and understood that my company and conversation were, at least momentarily, inferior to what you'd be having with her.

A few steps farther down the road, my flower hit the pavement. You picked it up, ceremoniously dismembered both your flower and mine, and gave my purple petals and bright yellow stamens back into my hand while you fisted yours.

You suggested that we each whisper three wishes into the petals in our hands and then throw them into the air. I wished for 1) a long life in health, 2) the physical and spiritual integrity of my children, and 3) a clear understanding of God's Word. I threw my hands up, and my petals and stamens disappeared. My ritual completed, I turned just in time to catch the delight on your face as your flower showered you.

We discussed if we could discuss what each of us wished for. You recommended and then decided for us that if the petals had touched us on the way down, then that freed us from the rules of secret wishes to tell each other one secret wish.

147

I shared that I had wished for my kids to be healthy and love God. What a coincidence! You shared that you had wished for me to get better.

We rounded the block and encountered our neighbor girls walking their new puppy. I made small talk and didn't notice until we had walked on past that you were crying. The rude puppy had scratched your hand when you had tried to pet it. I suggested that I bite your hand clean off so it would bleed for full effect or go back to inflict mortal wounds on the offending puppy. These choices brought a smile. Turned out that a kiss did the trick.

We stopped to admire the spring green fields and the verdant hills framed between the purple Table Rocks capped with the billowing blue sky. You sighed and said you wished our house had this view. Then you would wake up every morning, stretch and say, "Wow! That's beautiful!" after you put on your glasses.

"Now what should we talk about?" My ideas were fielded and sidelined politely, but how about we play the alphabet game with movies? We helped each other when we got stuck on hard letters that hadn't birthed many titles. Fortunately, wildlife movies came in handy for G (*Wildlife Gorillas*), K (*Wildlife Kangaroos*), and Q (*Wildlife Quails).* I had to acknowledge *Wildlife Quails* as a legitimate family favorite.

We turned into the homestretch holding hands again. The sun was cooling, slackening its hold on the day but still getting caught in strands of your blonde, flyaway ponytail. You were so unconscious of the verve you were exuding.

We reached the house, your attention transferred from me to your brother playing basketball, and the magic was arrested. We parted, as though nothing extraordinary had happened. I seized the front doorknob, buffeted by a wave of sentimentality, knowing what a tragically lost opportunity I would have suffered if I had gone on the walk alone.

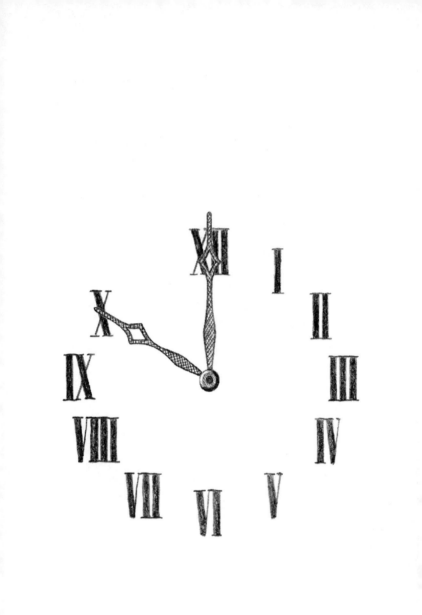

ten o'clock

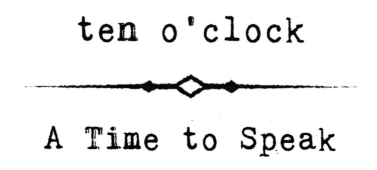

A Time to Speak

1.   Dusty book
       Hiding possibilities
       On the shelf
       Overlooked

2.   Words compiled on paper
       Bunched on the page trying
       To force a new thought

3.   Tryst with hero romancing
       My imagination
       I savor
       Last words as a kiss

4.   Light burns way past midnight
       Can't turn it off because I
       Can't lay it down.

5. Don't know recipe
    Find cookbook
    Don't know spelling
    Find dictionary

6. Story takes me far away
    Refuse the children,
    "Go out and play!
    Dinner will be late.
    Never mind! Get cereal."

7. Library fines are my privilege
    Checked it out but didn't read,
    Held on long past due date,
    Due to greed

8. I hoard a collection
    Of a time and a place:
    This one devoured in an airport,
    This one made me cry.
    I know just who would
    Appreciate this one

9. Authors assume authority
I agree or
wish I was their editor

10. Riding on a bus
Little girl with knees drawn up
Forty-five minutes
of assured relationship
with Dostoevsky or
Laura Ingalls Wilder

11. Good book with the golden rule
Gilded edges red word parade
Double-edged sword
Inflicts papercut
Conscience wounds
The Word becomes flesh and
Makes a home among us

12. Kind book open gently
Crisp pages represent hope
Small world just got bigger
Words find a home

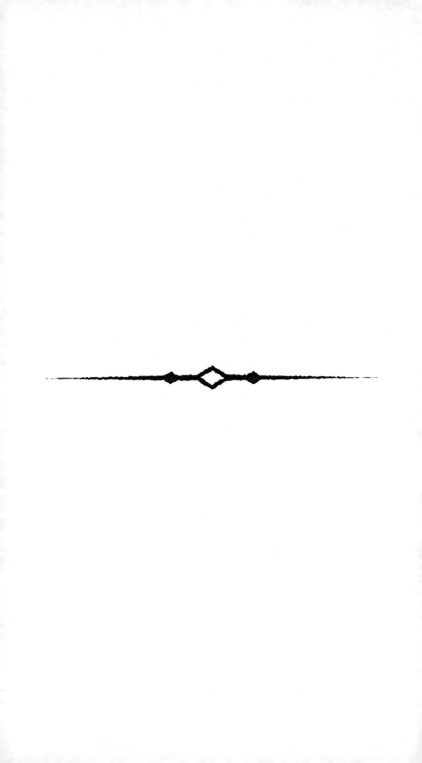

Unsaid

I cannot blame you for not asking
the perfect leading questions.
I saw being quiet as an invitation,
and you understood my silence
as a wall I hid behind,
or worse, to mean that I had nothing to say.

I had the words the whole time,
but I was cynical with them.
I wanted to say them out loud to you,
but in my mind, I saw your face
as my blurred words hit your understanding,
and I recoiled in abortive disappointment.

So I turn from spoken word to written,
but I have qualms here too.

I am afraid to write,
and I let fear dictate to me
about something I really enjoy.
I'm afraid that what I write
will either really suck or be really decent.
I'll be embarrassed either way
and probably not know the difference.

Words won't work if you don't want them to,
or if their meaning is lost,
or if they're stolen or unsaid.
But words are all I have,
so I have to get them to you.

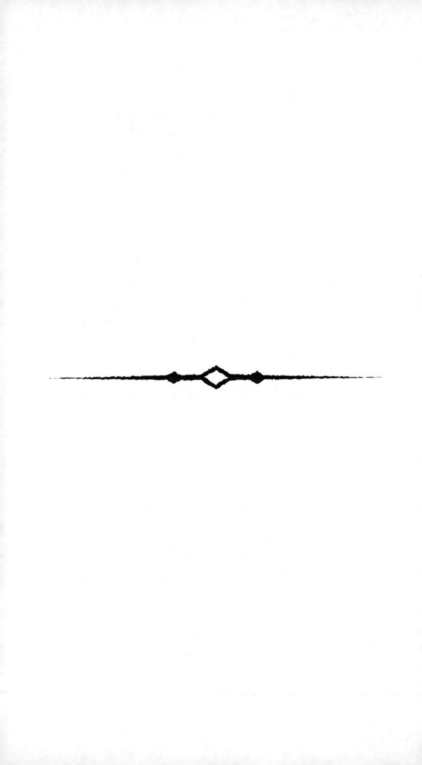

What I Meant to Say

I had something to say,
and I said it,
but you didn't hear it.

I tried to hang a song in the air,
but it dribbled off my tongue
and fell on the floor between us.
I picked it up and brushed it off,
but it was scrambled egg hash
and not a song anymore.

I wanted to state my resolve to change,
but it was a blunted sword
and conquered nothing.

I tried to groan a deeper meaning,
yet empty void collided with bankruptcy
and colluded with what?

I wanted to say something significant,
but I laughed at myself instead,
having a fond appreciation for the ridiculous.

I tried to tell you, "I'm sorry,"
but what a damned, stupid thing to say
when everyone already knows how sorry I am.

I wanted to ask, "Do you love me?"
but it barbwired in my throat.
I tried to yank it out,
but it dug bloody fingernails up my voice.

A brilliant word started its journey
up from my soles.
It caught arthritis in my knee
and cirrhosised in my liver,
but it still held my thought.
My heart told my mind to give this word
a free pass through my lips,
but my teeth are nasty anarchists
and gnashed the word.
It hid and died alone behind a festering tooth,
leaving an Ebenezer scar on my swollen cheek.

Woe to the blistering word!
The word my sole issued and my liver digested,
my heart promoted and my mind sanctioned,
yet it did not make it up the salmon ladder
to spawn through my teeth
so that you could know
this one brilliant word I had for you.

I am quiet now.

I have other words to say, but _____
    a) I doubt my audience.
    b) I doubt my meaning.
    c) I doubt my semantics.
    d) I doubt my delivery.

Brilliant words die their death
at the hands of the best of intentions.

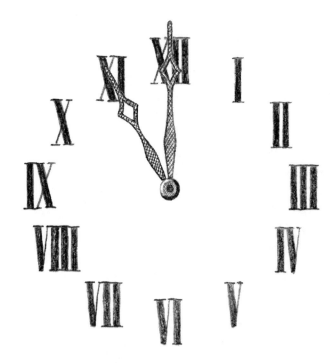

eleven o'clock

A Time to Be Silent

Wednesday
3:30 p.m.

I've wandered around this beautiful, holy place.
My first mute hour feels pressurized,
like I need to cough, but can't.
I feel rude and peculiar around others.
I haven't heard from my Father yet.
I'm resting now before the first prayer service,
trying to get comfortable in bed with solitude.

4:50 p.m.

Maybe I needed a nap.
The quiet in my room feels crisp and refreshing.
My window frames blue sky behind the bell tower.
The bells hang full of potential, poised and ready
for the next time they're called on to invoke.
I must hear the bells while I'm here,
even if I have to pull their ropes myself.

5:50 p.m.

I heard the bells, and my soul unlocked.
They gave flight to what I cannot say.
I have bowed. I have crossed myself.
I have listened to the monks' chant,
unchanged for millennia.
I go to partake of a listening meal.

6:45 p.m.

Dinner was delicious;
the view was bucolic;
the company was my own.
My smile is getting a run for its money
while I sit like a detentioned, ne're-do-well
in the far corner of the room.

What need does God have of us?
Are we truly a need
or the most tiresome way possible
for Him to accomplish His will on earth?
Would a rock do a finer job of praising Him than I?

7:05 p.m.

What can I do physically
that sets me apart spiritually?
Baptism, communion, the sacraments?
Dress differently, cover my head,
genuflect, eat kosher?
Can you have the Law without the Spirit?
Can you obey the Spirit without the Law?

9:00 p.m.

A life of discipline
apparently means not doing what I want,
against which my flesh is currently rebelling.
I have a mingled, drowsy sensation
of boredom and frustration.
I have so far to go.

I thought about N.T. Wright's opening thesis
in his book about the Psalms:
we are longing for places
where Law and Spirit intersect
at the crossroads of
temporal and eternal (`time`),
heaven and earth (`space`),
body and soul (`matter`).

These crossroads are truly the road less traveled,
the straight and narrow inconveniently located
near huge pitfalls of temptation.
The very places where we can transcend
into the Presence of God
are littered by distractive, destructive idols.

I can't describe how lovely this night is.
It's too much for me to take in.
O LORD, meet me in this place, this time, this body.
Meet me in the Psalms. Meet me in the dark.
Come gently. You know my weaknesses.
Make up for them.

Thursday
5:10 a.m.

The world and its Creator are too vast.
My soul is too finite.
I am in awe in Your Presence.
The loudest person here is in my head.
I can't turn off my self-talk.
Shut up!
LORD, help me still and quiet my mind.

Off to Vigils.

7:30 a.m.

I shall take possession of "coincidences"
as proof that God has come along beside me.

Yesterday before Vespers,
I prayed the LORD's Prayer,
not knowing what was before me
nor having anything better to say or pray.
The monks include that prayer in every Vespers.

Then at dinner last night,
a hummingbird lightly perched right beside me.
God often sends me birds as a sign of His Presence.

Last night, I read Luke 1:76-79 and Psalm 104.
In Lauds just now, Luke 1:67-80 and Psalm 104
were the *only* two Scripture passages read!
Coincidences? I think not!

8:50 a.m.

I just partook of the Holy Eucharist,
the body and the blood of the Lamb.
I can praise God
with music or without,
with sound or with silence,
with the assembly or alone.

The prayers and services
of these dedicated monks around the world
at all hours of the day
are playing their part to hold the darkness at bay.

12:30 p.m.

Noon prayers and lunch were wonderful.
I took a nap just before.
I'm enjoying the Psalms and songs so much more
since I figured out where we are in the psalter.
Now I can read along since
the chant is like deciphering a Scottish brogue.
Silence is much easier to me today because
I know a bit more of the lay of the land.
Except for the inane pleasantries
I would have normally offered,
I am only missing being able to ask, "Why?"
This reminds me of Merrick
and all her thoughtful questions.

5:05 p.m.

I enjoyed time at the library, the bookstore
and scavenging snacks to eat while I read
in the comfort of the cool basement
before coming back to my room for another nap,
from which I have just awoken.
So ends my first day and begins my second.

8:10 p.m.

I have not experienced a night like this
with so much ethereal beauty.
The sky is a luscious pink
with an orange ball of sun
set in a blue and purple backdrop
over the green hills and red-bricked Abbey.
The air is still and hushed and cool,
fragranced with what could be
if God reopened the Garden.

I went to Vespers, dinner and walked the path.
I cried and tried to quiet my mind.
Outer silence is easier than inner silence.
After Compline prayers, I finally experienced
several minutes of total silence
in the protected atmosphere of the abbey.
I know I will deeply miss this time, space, matter
and will joyfully anticipate my next encounter.

Friday
6:06 a.m.

Getting up for Vigils was against my will!
The rubber meets the road in
Discipleship 101—Freshman Orientation.
How can I achieve these practices out of obedience
but not as a work of the flesh?
Most difficult, indeed!
Shall I persevere or give up?

8:50 a.m.

I inserted myself again into Mass and Communion.
The wine still burns my throat.
I am reluctant to leave; I want to taste more.
God whispered, "Go!
I am with you always, even to the end of this age."
I cried back, "But LORD!
I am not always with You!"
He replied, "You can change that.
If one might dare to love Me,
I would be willing to suffer it all.
You are made in My image,
So you can love as I have first loved you."

10:30 a.m.

I just finished N.T. Wright's book on the Psalms.
Thoughtfully, God provided an available copy
for purchase in the abbey bookstore.
I bought it yesterday to replace my library copy
as a memento of this momentous time
and so I could mark passages with liberality.
His closing thesis is that the Psalms
have sustained worshippers of YHWH
for millennia and will continue to do so
as further testimony to His faithfulness.

11:00 a.m.

I'm trying to use my last hours wisely.
I made my bed and prayed for its next inhabitant.
Now I'm sitting in my favorite place in the library.
A monk had the audacity to be here already
so I'm sitting here with him in what I hope is
an unpresumptuous silence.

12:20 p.m.

My hummingbird is here with me again at lunch.
He seems to say,
"Go in peace and in lightness of heart."
Into Your hands I commit my spirit.

1:00 p.m.

It is finished.
Apparently talking is like riding a bike;
you don't have to think about speaking
as much as not speaking.
My first words were of gratitude to my hosts.

My family is coming for me,
and then I segue into soccer??
How do I usher this spiritual realm
into my daily grind?
How to explain this time to someone?
I want to share.
I want it as my sole-possession.

Until we meet at a crossroads again
and every day in between.

Thank you, Father.

I'm trying to read reverently, yet as fast as I can. My room is sparse and neat, but its windows open up to the eventide luxury of the bell tower's reign over the Abbey.

I am alone and hushed.

The only voice I hear is the words jumping off the pages, landing on my intellect. The only sound is the silence of the bells, tolling in my imagination.

My old chair is comfortable under the lamp.

I have my Bible unwieldy and weighty, open and balanced on my thighs. Above it hovers the Psalms book by Wright that I hold in my hands. I read,

"The whole world is filled with His glory."

I look up to the window for confirmation. The pre-dawn air slips in around the cracks in the pane and brings a breathless message:

"Yes, it's true."

I read that God is waiting to meet us at an intersection of space and time.

How convenient!

Today in this place I have space and time. Sometimes I have neither. All the ingredients crucial to meeting with Him I line up in the room with my books. I am consumed with waiting and fidget in surging expectancy.

The belfry cracks open.

The first bell speaks, then is answered by its companions, not open to judgement.

Just glory.

I put my books down and stand. In this space and time under the bells beside my books in this reverberating silence,

I am with God.

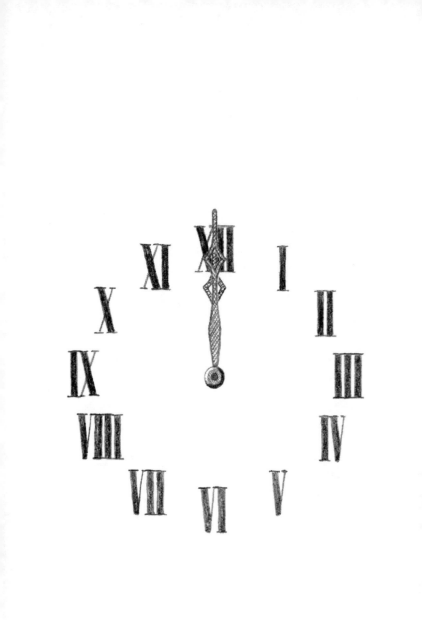

twelve o'clock

A Time for Peace

Insatiable

What makes you swallow
delicious food?

What makes you come apart
when loving is good?

What makes you exhale
when the air is so fresh?

What makes a baby bird
leave the comfort of nest?

All good things must come to an end.
Time brings the rhythm to courageously contend.

So we swallow and hope to follow
with another tasty bite.

We come together again
after a staged and epic fight.

Spent breath is needed
for contentedly sighing.

The little bird somehow knows
the nest prevents his flying.

Welcome, Rejected!

Open Closed
Sideways Silly
Salt and Pepper
Hot and Chilly
Bloated Float
Blindly Gloat

Righteous Sinner
Blight and Shiny
Snot-Nosed Brat
Mealy Whiny
Brave Coward
Craves Cold Power

Welcome, Rejected!
Purple Bruise
Heights and Depths
Lightning Cruise
Time and Space
True Basket Case

Pardoned Sinner
Right and Shiny
Homeless Homebody
Adopted Kindly
Thy Kingdom Come
Thy Will Be Done

Swim Toward Nobility

Part 1:   The Invitation

Cool and undisturbed,
the invitation lay open.
It stated simply, "Join me."

What to do, what to do
with such a chimerical possibility?
When was the last time
I made myself available to experience
the proper warmth of the unknown,
something outside my imagined control?

An unwished for slackening
on the reigns of control
had spirited this invitation
to me in the first place.

I choose to stop resisting.

I dive into the invitation.

Part 2:   The Acceptance

The water of joining you
splashed cold in my gut.
I jerked to the surface
to suck in my first breath of surprise,
And then it happened:
I felt an electric joy!

You swam toward me laughing;
each water droplet on your face
reflecting my unpretentious, girlish grin.

"What do we do now?" I asked,
harkening back to the trenches of routine.
My question disappointed you.
You hoped it would be obvious to me.

"Live. Just live.
Swim toward nobility,
and stay with me."

When God names Himself to Moses
He only uses one feminine Hebrew adjective:

True

That's all we get, ladies.
I feel honored and short-changed.

We were the last to be created,
post mealworm and hyena.
A second-class afterthought
or a crowning achievement?
The mathematical mystery of
equal but less than.

Yet we will be maintained through childbirth.

Because I have breasts,
I will use them to nurse
the undernourished realization
of who I am:

Faithful

And give birth to an aspect
of who God is.

Suppose I Made God My Idol

The made becomes the maker.
The maker prays to the made.
Then one bright person
with one right goal
goes and cuts down
their Asherah pole.

Suppose I sacrificed my son and daughters
       on the altar of allegiance to You,
       instead of handing them over
       to the negligent whims of self-gratification.

Suppose I burned the priests' incense
       of prayer to the One who can save,
       instead of bankrupting my hopes
       on chance and fortune.

Suppose I fell tumultuously in love with You
       and cheated on all the rest
       instead of prostituting my heart
       for a transient blush.

Suppose I was one bright person
       with one right goal
       and I cut down
       my Asherah pole.

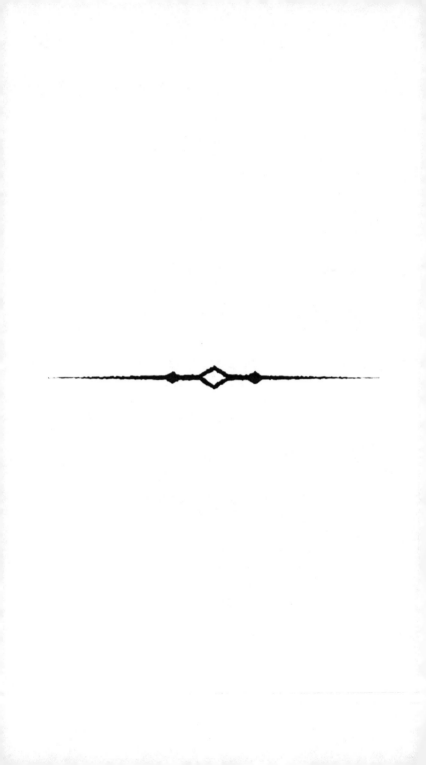

Picture of Me

The picture of me I like best
is the picture God has of me.

The picture of me
He keeps in a jeweled frame
He engraved with my true name.

The picture of me
He rests on His nightstand
close to Him on His right hand.

This picture of me hides none of my faults:

my glasses are crooked,
my smile is crooked,
my freckles debate whether they're moles,
my nose turns up at the end
like an upside down ski slope,

but my eyes—my eyes are magnificent.
You've never seen anything like them.

They're looking up at Him,
and you can see in them
what He means to me.

The picture of me I like best
is the picture God has of me.

Hallebloomjah

I will bloom as an old gnarled tree,
in my prime past my prime,
not as I thought I ought to be,
but a lovely bloom that bursts out of time.

I will bloom in an old sacred swamp,
wearing a halo of lilies on hallowed ground.
A heron will rest on my cypress knee stump.
The Spanish moss sways like my hair let down.

I will bloom from a forgotten sunflower seed
left on the sun-swept, wind-scorched field,
facing the sky's glory as my volunteer deed,
lost on the dirt, yet expected to yield.

I will bloom lying flat on the sea,
blooming in time to do God's glory a favor,
a human starfish that only He can see,
ready to accept the kiss of Jonah's savior.

I have found You when I jumped
off the roof into snow—
in that free fall, safely caught memory.

I have found You broody over my contented night
when the fat moon shone on my bedroom wall,
and I couldn't think of one thing wrong.

I have found You in my ugly, pink, flowered
Bible cover Delphia gave me
on my thirteenth birthday.
I still carry You around in it
like the old lady I've always been.

I have found You floating above
the standing army of a ripe wheat field,
shuffling in its spiny armor,
waiting to be cut down.

I have found You sitting beside me on a rock wall
listening to ancient dust settle on olive leaves,
the air so much older on the other
side of the planet where Your church began.

I have found You in a baby's kiss,
that somehow not revolting recipe
of drool and snot and milk crustaceans.

I have found You in my dreams.
"Come, follow Me," You said,
leading the way in light.

I have found You in the bottles of wine
poured at our Passover meal.
I lit the candles.
Were You at the door?
I thought I saw You.

I have found You in the birds
I know You sent to me:
the hummingbird inspired
to hover parallel to our horror,
the red cardinal I've never seen
before or since that terrible day;

I have found You where the veil is thinner,
dwelling with Your people, confessing Your name.

I have found You walking among words, each one
tripping over itself to make You understood.

I have found You in a meal brought to the board
from a cow's udder, dirt, sun and strong hands.

I have found You where
I thought You wouldn't be:
in my pain and uncertainty.
You were there.
I just wanted more of You and less of me.

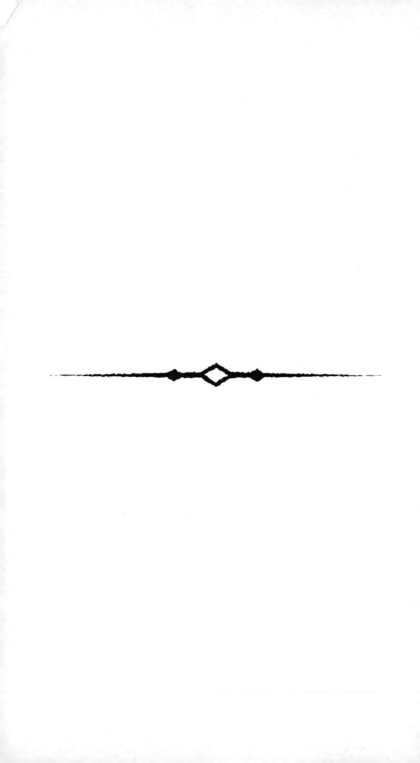